ARCHITECTURE TOURS L.A. GUIDEBOOK
DOWNTOWN

ARCHITECTURE TOURS L.A. GUIDEBOOK
DOWNTOWN

LAURA MASSINO SMITH

Schiffer Publishing Ltd
4880 Lower Valley Road, Atglen, PA 19310 USA

Library of Congress Cataloging-in-Publication Data

Smith, Laura Massino.
    Architecture tours L.A. guidebook:downtown/by Laura Massino Smith.
        p. cm.
    ISBN 0-7643-2084-X (pbk.)
1. Architecture—California—Los Angeles—Tours.
2. Los Angeles (Calif.)—Buildings, structures, etc.—Tours. I. Title: Downtown.
    II. Title
NA735.L55S55 2004
720' .9794'94—dc22   2004006094

Designed by John P. Cheek
Type set in Futura BdCn BT/Humanist 521 LT BT
ISBN: 0-7643-2084-X
Printed in China
1 2 3 4

DEDICATION

To my extraordinary husband, Drew, whose undying love, patience, encouragement, and support have guided me to discover my true passion.

Published by Schiffer Publishing Ltd.
4880 Lower Valley Road
Atglen, PA 19310
Phone: (610) 593-1777; Fax: (610) 593-2002
E-mail: Info@schifferbooks.com

For the largest selection of fine reference books on this and related subjects, please visit our web site at www.schifferbooks.com
We are always looking for people to write books on new and related subjects. If you have an idea for a book please contact us at the above address.

This book may be purchased from the publisher.
Include $3.95 for shipping.
Please try your bookstore first.
You may write for a free catalog.

In Europe, Schiffer books are distributed by
Bushwood Books
6 Marksbury Ave.
Kew Gardens
Surrey TW9 4JF England
Phone: 44 (0) 20 8392-8585; Fax: 44 (0) 20 8392-9876
E-mail: info@bushwoodbooks.co.uk
Free postage in the U.K., Europe; air mail at cost.

Architecture Tours L.A.

www.architecturetoursla.com
323.464.7868

Architecture Tours L.A. specializes in guided driving tours led by an architectural historian in a 1962 vintage Cadillac. Our tours focus on the historic and significant contemporary architecture in Los Angeles, highlighting the cultural aspects of the history of the city's built environment. This guidebook will allow you to drive yourself and discover L.A. in your own car, at your own pace. In addition to DOWNTOWN, other tours offered by Architecture Tours L.A. include:

HOLLYWOOD
HANCOCK PARK/MIRACLE MILE
WEST HOLLYWOOD/BEVERLY HILLS
SILVER LAKE
PASADENA
FRANK GEHRY

Disclaimer

It is not advisable for anyone operating a motor vehicle to read this book. Please pull your car into a safe, designated parking area before attempting any fine print. Better yet, take this tour with a friend who can act as navigator and narrator. Naturally, the best way to see it all is riding shotgun with the author!

Neither the author nor the publisher assume responsibility for moving violations committed while intoxicated by this tour.

Note to Tour-Goers

The sites included in this self-guided tour represent the architectural highlights of the DOWNTOWN area. This tour is meant to be an overview, a starting point of sorts, and is intended to give the participant a feeling for the neighborhood. By no means does the tour include everything of interest. Numerous books of ponderous proportions have been written to that end, and if your interest is piqued, you might refer to the bibliography in the back of this book for further reading.

Herein, within a matter of hours you will glean a pretty good understanding of what historically happened, and what is currently happening architecturally in DOWNTOWN. The photographs herein are for quick identification of what you will be seeing up close, in full scale.

The Downtown area of Los Angeles is one of the few areas of the city that can be seen very well on foot because so much of the architecture is found very close together. For this tour in particular, we recommend that you park the car and walk in areas of particular interest to get even better views of the details on the buildings. Also, many of the commercial buildings on this tour are accessible to the public and can be seen from inside. The criteria for inclusion into this guidebook consist of the historical, cultural, and architectural significance of each site, and the fact that it can be seen relatively easily from the street. So relax and have a great ride!

INTRODUCTION

One of the most architecturally diverse areas in all of southern California, Downtown Los Angeles is home to some of the oldest and newest structures in the city. This is truly the historic core of the city, where the first inhabitants settled and where some of the most important buildings were built, including City Hall and Union Station.

Los Angeles was founded in 1781 by the Spanish explorers who discovered the Tongva Indians living close to the Los Angeles River. Colonization of the area began when families from Mexico were sent to found the city of Los Angeles. A village was centered around Downtown L.A. very near the Civic Center, Olvera Street, and the Pueblo de Los Angeles. The oldest surviving buildings in Los Angeles are located in and around Olvera Street—starting with the oldest house, the Avila Adobe, c. 1818, which can only be seen from the pedestrian street. The surrounding buildings, including the church, hotel, firehouse, and others, now comprise a living museum, as the Plaza is the location for many present day celebrations, festivals, and everyday activities.

In 1876 the completion of the Southern Pacific Railroad route to Los Angeles from the East and Midwest, in conjunction with a railroad price war led to the mass migration of people who wanted to take advantage of the last frontier and the great climate. Large immigrant populations from France, Germany, Spain, Mexico, Italy, Syria, China, and other countries who were all living Downtown formed labor forces that built the city and the rail lines.

Much of what is seen Downtown today represents a second or third building in the same location. All of Downtown was at one time lined with wooden Victorian buildings built during the mid-to-late 1800s. During the economic boom of the 1880s, the wealthiest Angelenos moved to Bunker Hill (the current location of California Plaza and MOCA), where they built magnificent Victorian mansions. Many have been demolished, but some still remain on the outskirts of town, as you will see at the end of the tour.

Another of the many faces of Downtown were oil wells. During the early 1900s oil wells stood and pumped as much oil as they could from the land. In the 1920s there was another economic boom, and much of what you see today along Seventh Street and Broadway, in particular, were built at that time. The Art Deco style was fully expressed here, and can be seen in all of its exuberance in establishments such as the Eastern Columbia Building and the Oviatt Building. Arguably the most important building of the 1930s was Union Station (1939), bringing more people from all over into the City of Angels. Although it displaced the original Chinatown to where it is now located, Union Station stands as a symbol of mobility. The next economic boom came after World War II, when many of the suburbs surrounding Los Angeles, including the San Fernando Valley, were built. Urban renewal schemes of the 1960s and 1970s saw the demolition of more of the city's older structures in order to make room for skyscrapers, which continue to go up today.

A strong preservation movement also started in the late 1970s by the Los Angeles Conservancy, which saved many of the historic structures from demolition. Today, these historic buildings are enjoying a resurgence of interest in their conversions to apartments, lofts, or schools.

The Library Tower is the tallest building west of the Mississippi. It was built in 1989 across from the Central Library, which was built in 1926 and was the first historic structure to be saved from demolition by the Los Angeles Conservancy. Other structures were built in L.A. during the 1990s, and in the new century we already have two impressive structures by world-renowned architects—the Cathedral of Our Lady of the Angels, 2002, and The Walt Disney Concert Hall, 2003. Currently, the balance of the preservation of important historic buildings and the creation of new important buildings seems just right.

250 South Grand Avenue Between 1st and 3rd Streets

1) Museum of Contemporary Art (MOCA), 1986, Arata Isozaki with Gruen Associates, 250 SOUTH GRAND AVENUE

1) We start here at the Museum of Contemporary Art (MOCA), a relatively young museum with an excellent collection of modern and contemporary art. The building was designed by Japanese architect Arata Isozaki. It was designed in the Post-modern era and uses geometric forms and glass pyramid skylights to let indirect natural light into the galleries. The main exhibition galleries are located below street level, while the offices and museum shop are at street level. The exterior is clad in red Indian stone.

2) Next door to MOCA you'll find a very new structure that houses The Colburn School of Performing Arts for music and dance. It is yet another gem in the "Cultural Corridor," as Grand Avenue is now referred to, for obvious reasons. The Zipper Concert Hall is housed here. Zinc scales on the roof, brick walls, wood, and Plexiglas comprise the structure. Inside is the studio designed by Lloyd Wright in 1946 for the violinist Jascha Heifetz. The firm that designed this building also designed the new addition to the Los Angeles County Museum of Art, which was completed in 1985, and the expansion of the Central Library just down the street, in 1993.

2) The Colburn School of Performing Arts, 1998, Hardy Holzman Pfeiffer Associates, 200 SOUTH GRAND AVENUE

3) On your left is the Walt Disney Concert Hall, which is visible from all four sides. Designed by Canadian-born local architect Frank O. Gehry, the design was first revealed in 1987 after it was chosen from a design competition. Lillian Disney, the widow of Walt Disney, donated the original $50 million for the hall, and real estate developer/ philanthropist Eli Broad raised the remainder needed for completion. Work was halted for a time due to lack of funds and a falling out between the architect and the firm producing the working drawings. Attached to a 14,000-piece structural steel skeleton, the exterior is comprised of 6,400 stainless steel and 3,000 polished steel panels. The building's highly amorphous and sculptural design was worked out on a computer with Catia software, which is used to design aircraft. Gehry wanted this to be "a flower for Lillian" because she loved flowers. He also wanted "a living room for Los Angeles." He is interested in the movement of the city and explores how this building fits into that movement. Indeed, this building is full of movement, as the large curved forms resemble sails on a ship. The movement is created in the dramatic sweeps of steel through the air. Gehry has created "architecture as art" and has added a beautiful sculpture in the middle of the city. This is one of the most unique buildings in the city, and is the home of the Los Angeles Philharmonic, the Los Angeles Master Chorale, and the Redcat Theater.

3) Walt Disney Concert Hall, 2003, Frank O. Gehry & Associates, SOUTH GRAND AVENUE AND 1ST STREET

4) On the far corner, the tan colored structure is the Los Angeles County Courthouse, designed by a group of architects for a design competition. Housed here are the county courts and related offices. This is a typical municipal building of the late 1950s. You will get other views as you go.

4) Los Angeles County Courthouse, 1958, J.E. Stanton, Paul Williams, Adrian Wilson, Austin, Field and Fry, CORNER HILL & 1ST STREET

Left on 1st Street

5) From the fundraising efforts of Dorothy Chandler, wife of the *L.A. Times* publisher from 1944-1960, Norman Chandler, the Music Center was born, thus creating a cultural center where "Broadway"-type productions are staged. The Center is also home to the Los Angeles Opera. The Dorothy Chandler Pavilion on the 1st Street side was the former home of the Los Angeles Philharmonic, and over the years some of the Academy Awards presentations were held here. It is an elegant building topped by a flat overhanging roof to shield the soaring glass walls, which are slightly curved on two sides. In the middle is the Mark Taper Forum, a circular building faced with an abstract relief sculpture and surrounded by a shallow pool. This is where some of the more avant-garde plays are presented. At the opposite end, on the Temple Street side, is the Ahmanson Theater, named after the Home Savings banking family. Many productions from Broadway in New York City come here. In the center is a large plaza with a fountain and various sculptures; the parking garage is underground.

6) A beautifully striking building set back on the site, giving it room to stand. A reflecting pool also serves to let it stand alone. The white horizontal banding emphasizes the layers (floors) and makes a strong geometric statement.

6) Department of Water & Power Headquarters, 1965, Albert C. Martin & Associates, 111 NORTH HOPE STREET

5) Performing Arts Center of Los Angeles (formerly known as the Music Center), 1969, Welton Becket & Associates, Comprising: The Dorothy Chandler Pavilion, The Ahmanson Theatre, and The Mark Taper Forum, GRAND AVENUE BETWEEN TEMPLE AND 1ST STREETS

**Left on Hope Street
Left on Kosciusko
under MOCA
Right on Hill St.**

7) On your left is the back of Subway Terminal Building. An extensive streetcar system traveled from Hollywood, the San Fernando Valley, the beaches, and into Downtown L.A. during the 1920s to the early 1960s. The system went underground for about a mile to relieve congestion on the streets of Downtown, and this is where it terminated. At the very top of the building notice the tromp l'oeuil windows that complete the window fenestration pattern. The building has been declared a Historic Cultural Monument by the City of Los Angeles.

7) (Back of) Subway Terminal Building, 1926, Schultze & Weaver
Restored 1986, Levin & Associates, 417 SOUTH HILL STREET

8) The latest incarnation of Pershing Square, this was once a traditional Beaux-Arts city square with lush gardens and wrought-iron and wood benches. Some of the traditional elements have been retained, however, re-interpreted in a Post-modern fashion. Notice the tall bell tower painted deep purple. On the opposite side are earthy-pink truncated columns—another re-interpretation of a Classical form for the late 20th century. Mexican in origin, Legoretta is informed by the colors of Mexico, and so here we see earthy purple bell towers, yellow walls, and dusty-pink columns. Still remaining from the original square is a statue of General John J. Pershing and a cannon from the warship Constitution, a.k.a. "Old Ironsides."

8) Pershing Square, 1994, Ricardo Legorreta & Hanna/Olin, OLIVE & 5TH, HILL & 6TH STREETS

9) On your right is The Gas Company, designed in the shape of a stylized glass flame with the building around it. You will see better views as you get further away. However, if you look straight up, you will see the curved glass which comes to a sharp point on either end. This is the flame-shaped logo of the Gas Company incorporated literally and physically into the building.

9) The Gas Company, 1991, Richard Keating, (Skidmore, Owings & Merrill), 555 WEST 5TH STREET

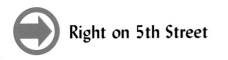

Right on 5th Street

10) On your left you will see the Biltmore Hotel, which was designed by the same architects as the Subway Terminal Building here and the Waldorf-Astoria Hotel in New York. It was designed in a combination of styles, including the European Beaux-Arts style with elements of Italian Renaissance and Spanish Churriguerresque. In 1986, the building was restored and remodeled. One of the grandest hotels in L.A., the building has been declared a Historic Cultural Monument by the City of Los Angeles.

10) (Regal) Biltmore Hotel, 1923, Schultze & Weaver, 506 SOUTH GRAND AVENUE, (515 SOUTH OLIVE AVENUE)

11) Southern California Edison Building (now One Bunker Hill), 1931, Allison & Allison, 601 WEST 5TH STREET

11) On your right is the original Southern California Edison Building in the Art Deco style. Its very block-like form was typical of the 1930s Art Deco style. Murals on the interior depict power and light. Now used as an office building, the building has been declared a Historic Cultural Monument by the City of Los Angeles.

12) This is recognized as the tallest building west of the Mississippi. Of quasi-cylindrical, geometric shape with angled green glass windows, it has seventy-five floors and a granite façade. There is a mural on the interior by Russian artists Vitaly Komar and Alexander Melamid. Three thousand people work here in various offices, and the Herman Miller furniture showroom is also located here.

13) On your right are the Bunker Hill Steps. Fashioned after the Spanish Steps in Rome, they feature a cascading fountain running down the center. Water emanates from the top of the steps, out of a sculpture by Robert Graham called "Water Source."

14) On your left, you'll see the Central Library, which was burned in two arson fires in the mid-1980s and was restored and expanded in 1993. Its design is a combination of Spanish, Egyptian, Byzantine, and modern architecture. Notice the mosaic pyramid at the top. When this building was threatened, the Los Angeles Conservancy, L.A.'s main preservation organization, was formed to save it from demolition. This building has been declared a Historic Cultural monument by the City of Los Angeles. It is also listed on the National Register of Historic Places.

13) Bunker Hill Steps, 1990, Lawrence Halprin, WEST 5TH STREET

12) First Interstate World Center (now Library Tower), 1989, Henry Cobb; Pei, Cobb, Freed & Partners/Harold Fredenburg, 633 WEST 5TH STREET

14) Central Library, 1926, Bertram Goodhue, Restoration and expansion, 1993, Hardy Holzman Pfeiffer Associates, 630 WEST 5TH STREET

15) The Westin Bonaventure Hotel on the far right corner is comprised of a grouping of glass cylinders. The mirrored cylindrical composition creates dynamic spaces inside, as well as reflecting the surrounding buildings on the exterior. Note the exterior elevators that are like fast-moving thrill rides in an amusement park. On one of the top floors is a lounge with a revolving floor that completes one revolution in about 1 1/4 hours. From here the views of the city are excellent.

15) Westin Bonaventure Hotel, 1976, John Portman, 404 SOUTH FIGUEROA STREET

 **Left on Flower Street**

16) On your right as you turn the corner is the Atlantic Richfield (Arco) Plaza. This was designed by the same architects who created the DWP building seen earlier. The structure is basically composed of two, large granite boxes with square windows. In the building's central plaza is a red sculpture in a double helix form called "Double Ascension."

In this spot there was once a magnificent Art Deco Moderne style building, built in 1928 by Morgan, Walls, and Clements, which was unfortunately demolished.

16) Atlantic Richfield (Arco) Plaza, 1972, Albert C. Martin & Associates, "Double Ascension", 1973 (sculpture), Herbert Bayer, 515 SOUTH FLOWER STREET

17) On your left is The California Club, a private social organization started in the late 1890s. The structure was designed in the neo-Classical style, or the Beaux-Arts style, and surfaced with brown Roman brick. The building has been declared a Historic Cultural Monument by the City of Los Angeles.

17) The California Club, 1930, Robert D. Farquhar, 238 SOUTH FLOWER STREET

18) Further on your left, you'll see what was once the site of the Superior Oil Company's headquarters. The original structure has been retained and transformed into a trendy hotel with a rooftop pool, bar, and very lively party scene. The exterior is faced with vertical bands of Carrara white-and-black marble and stainless steel spandrels. The building has been declared a Historic Cultural Monument by the City of Los Angeles. It is also listed on the National Register of Historic Places.

19) On the left is the California Counties Gas Company Building, in the Romanesque Revival and Beaux-Arts styles. The entrance is marked by engaged columns within three large arches decorated with acanthus foliage, shield shapes, scrolling, and leaf patterns, with more arches and columns at the top. Once an office building, it is currently being converted to apartments.

18) Superior Oil Company (now Standard Hotel), 1956, Claude Beelman, Remodeled 2002, Koning-Eizenberg, 550 SOUTH FLOWER STREET

19) California Counties Gas Company Building, c. 1924, (architect unknown), 810 SOUTH FLOWER STREET

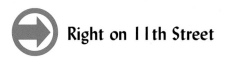

Right on 11th Street

20) Resembling the prow of an ocean liner, this building looks as though it could charge right up Figueroa Street. The Los Angeles Lakers basketball team plays here, and large pop concerts are held here.

20) Staples Arena, 1999, NBBJ, FIGUEROA AT 11TH

21) On your left, behind the Staples Arena, you'll see the Los Angeles Convention Center at South Figueroa Street. Constructed in 1972, it was first designed by Charles Luckman Associates, and then remodeled in 1980 and 1993 by Pei, Cobb, and Freed & Partners with Gruen Associates. It hosts gatherings of all kinds. The interior floor has an interesting map of the world designed into the tilework.

21) Los Angeles Convention Center, 1993, Pei, Cobb, Freed & Partners with Gruen Associates, 1201 SOUTH FIGUEROA STREET

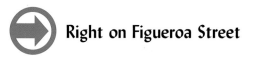

Right on Figueroa Street

22) On your left, The Hotel Figueroa has a Moroccan theme façade, which is carried on into the interior lobby.

22) Hotel Figueroa, 1925, Stanton, Reed, and Hibbard, 939 SOUTH FIGUEROA STREET

23) On your right is the Friday Morning Club Building, designed in the European Beaux-Arts style with elements of Byzantine architecture, such as the decoration on the columns and decorative diamond pattern. Characteristics of Romanesque architecture are apparent, such as the repeated arches throughout the façade. This was originally the home of a women's charitable organization, and is now a performance space. The building has been declared a Historic Cultural Monument by the City of Los Angeles. It is also listed on the National Register of Historic Places.

24) A city legend on your left, the Original Pantry Cafe is a greasy spoon restaurant if ever there was one. It began very humbly with only one room, a few stools, a little grill, hot plate, and sink. It is open twenty-four hours and apparently has quite a following, because every Saturday and Sunday mornings a long line of people wait on the sidewalk to get in for breakfast! Partly owned by former L.A. mayor Richard Riordan, the building has been declared a Historic Cultural Monument by the City of Los Angeles.

25) The tall, elegant white structure on the left is the 777 Tower, which was designed by the Argentinean architect who also designed the Pacific Design Center in West Hollywood, and many other buildings around the world. Resembling a tall wedding cake, it elegantly steps back as it rises with everted rims crowning each section. The curved façade also softens its appearance as it faces Figueroa Street.

23) Friday Morning Club Building (now Variety Arts Center), 1924, Allison & Allison, 940 SOUTH FIGUEROA STREET

24) Original Pantry Café, 1924, (architect unknown), 877 SOUTH FIGUEROA STREET

25) 777 Tower, 1991, Cesar Pelli & Associates, 777 FIGUEROA STREET

Right on Seventh Street

Originally farmlands, then residences and schools from the 1880s, by the early 1900s Seventh Street was the main shopping district in Los Angeles and was originally lined with department stores, some of which still remain intact.

26) Home Savings of America Tower (now Figueroa Tower), 1989, Albert C. Martin & Associates, 660 SOUTH FIGUEROA STREET

26) On your left at the corner is the Home Savings of America Tower. Designed in the Historic Eclectic Post-modern style, re-interpreting and updating Classical architecture, it borrows from a French Chateauesque tower, which resembles the Plaza Hotel in New York. The top of the steeply sloped Chateauesque roof is best seen from a distance. The gold and grey striping of the lower floors borrows from Byzantine architecture.

27) Barker Brothers Building, 1925, Curlett & Beelman, 818 WEST 7TH STREET

27) On your right at the corner, the building with the enormous central arched entrance is the former Barker Brothers furniture store designed in the Italian Renaissance Revival style, which originated in the 17th century and was a return to the Classical forms. It is characterized by the large, rusticated-stone ground floor level, arched doorways and windows, and flat roofs with crowning cornice and modillion bracketing. This building was modeled after the Strozzi Palace in Florence, Italy. Barker Brothers left the building in 1984, and it has since been renovated and is for use as offices on the upper floors and retail on the ground floor. The building has been declared a Historic Cultural Monument by the City of Los Angeles.

28) The Fine Arts Building across the street was designed in the Romanesque Revival style, and is one of the most unique buildings in the city. Elaborately decorated with repeating twisted columns that flank the central arched entrance, notice the representations of flora, fauna, and gargoyles, which are all made of terra cotta, completing a phantasmagoric theme. It was originally built for artists' studios, with an elaborate lobby featuring display cases to showcase their art. The walls of the lobby are detailed in tile and rusticated terra cotta block. The terra cotta was provided by Batchelder Studios. Ernest Batchelder supervised the creation of the exterior sculptures representing Architecture, Painting, Textile Arts, and Ceramics. Developer Ratkovich & Bowers renovated the building in 1986 with Levin & Associates. The building has been declared a Historic Cultural Monument by the City of Los Angeles.

29) On the left, the Roosevelt Building was also designed in the Italian Renaissance Revival style, similar to the Barker Brothers Building, by the same architects, but with three central arches instead of one, and was originally used for offices as it is now. The façade is comprised of rusticated terra cotta. The building has been declared a Historic Cultural Monument by the City of Los Angeles.

29) Roosevelt Building (now 7th Street Metro Center), 1925,
Curlett & Beelman, 727 West 7th Street

28) Fine Arts Building, 1927, Walker & Eisen, Restored 1986, Levin & Associates, 811 West 7th Street

30) On the right is the former Boston Dry Goods/J.W. Robinson Company. Proprietor Joseph Winchester Robinson was from Boston. Robinson's Department Store started as Boston Dry Goods in 1883, and opened at this location in 1915. What remains is the newer (1934) remodeling by Mayberry, Allison & Allison, surfaced in glazed terra cotta tile and designed in the Late Art Deco Moderne style popular in the 1930s. Robinson's grew to be a major department store in southern California, and still exists today. The building has been declared a Historic Cultural Monument by the City of Los Angeles.

30) Boston Dry Goods/J.W. Robinson Company, 1915, Frederick Noonan & William Richards, Remodeled 1934, Mayberry, Allison & Allison, 600 West 7th Street

31) On the right at the far corner of 7th & Grand is Brooks Brothers. It was built in the early 1900s, making it one of the oldest buildings on 7th Street. This is a Classical Beaux-Arts style building that now houses offices and may be converted to living spaces.

31) Brooks Brothers, 1912, Harrison Albright/ Barnett, Haynes & Barnett, SE CORNER 7TH & GRAND

32) On the left was once Brock's Jewelers, once considered the "Tiffany's of California." An upscale jewelry store, it became Clifton's Cafeteria in 1974. The style is a mixture of Classical elements, such as the broken pediment at the top edged with scroll forms, and Churrigueresque details, including the highly decorated columns and spandrels. The building has been declared a Historic Cultural Monument by the City of Los Angeles.

32) Cliftons Silver Spoon Cafeteria (originally Brock & Company Jewelry Store), 1922, Dodd & Richards, 515 WEST 7TH STREET

33) Giannini Bank of Italy/Bank of America (now Giannini Place), 1922, Morgan, Walls & Morgan, 649 SOUTH OLIVE AVENUE

33) Next on the left is the Giannini Place, designed in the neo-Classical style. Resembling early Greek and Roman structures, on the ground floor, the fluted columns with Corinthian capitals create a sense of power and strength. The upper floors are much more pared-down. The building has been declared a Historic Cultural Monument by the City of Los Angeles.

34) Next on the left at the far corner is the Los Angeles Athletic Club, designed in the Beaux-Arts style with pressed block trimmed in terracotta, and a projecting metal cornice. There is a swimming pool on the sixth floor, with a track circling the pool and a skylight above. The club exists today as a center of Downtown sports and social activities. There are sporting trophies dating from 1904. Seventy-five club members have earned Olympic medals and many others have taken part in the Olympic games over the years. The building has been declared a Historic Cultural Monument by the City of Los Angeles.

 Left on Olive (weekends only, no left turn on weekdays. On weekdays, continue straight on 7th Street and proceed to the Pantages Theater on the left corner)

35) On the left is the Oviatt Building, one of the most elegant buildings in the city. Restored in 1980 by Levin & Associates, it was originally built as a men's store that was thought to be very chic and contemporary, due to the Art Deco details. Lalique glass was originally used in the ceiling of the lobby, but most has now been replaced. Mr. Oviatt had traveled to Paris and wanted to recreate what he saw there. Supposedly everything was designed and built in France and then brought here to be put together by imported French architects. Mr. Oviatt also had a rooftop apartment designed in the Art Deco style. This is currently the home of Cicada Restaurant, one of the best Italian restaurants in the city. The building has been declared a Historic Cultural Monument by the City of Los Angeles. It is also listed on the National Register of Historic Places.

34) Los Angeles Athletic Club, 1912, John Parkinson and Edwin Bergstrom, 431 WEST 7TH STREET

35) Oviatt Building, 1928, Walker & Eisen, Restored 1980, Levin & Associates, 617 SOUTH OLIVE STREET

Map Three

Right on 6th Street
Right on Hill Street

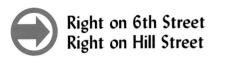

36) View of Pershing Square with bell tower visible.

37) On the right corner is the former Pantages/Warner Brothers Theater, designed by the same architect who designed the well-known and still operating Pantages Theater on Hollywood Blvd. as well as others. Alexander Pantages was a successful theater developer and had theaters built all over this country. Beaux-Arts in style, the building addresses the busy intersection with its rounded corner and the richly ornamented walls continue down both streets. Fluted columns and highly decorated images of vines and heroic female forms adorn the terra cotta façade. In 1929 the theater was purchased by Warner Brothers and opened as the Warner Brothers Downtown Theater. They began to exhibit the latest innovation in the motion picture industry, film with sound, a.k.a. "Talkies," which came out in 1927. The Jewelry Mart now operates as part of the wholesale Jewelry District, however, it is possible to walk through and see where the original stage and seats of the theater were. It is also possible to see some of the remaining high style details.

37) Pantages/Warner Brothers Theater, 1920, Benjamin Marcus Priteca, 401-421 WEST 7TH STREET

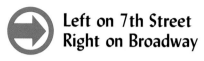

Left on 7th Street
Right on Broadway

Here on Broadway is the Historic Theater District, which is listed on the National Register of Historic Places. Up and down Broadway was the largest concentration of movie theaters in the world during the 1930s. This was once the central entertainment area of Los Angeles. Some of these theaters were originally built for Vaudeville and now most are used for other purposes, mostly retail. Currently the area is a thriving Latino commercial district.

38) On the left, the Globe Theater was designed in the Classical Beaux-Arts style, and originally staged dramatic shows instead of Vaudeville, which was popular at that time. In the 1930s, however, the theater began to show movies. In 1987 it was converted to a store.

38) Globe Theater (also known as The Morosco Theater), 1921, Morgan and Walls, 744 SOUTH BROADWAY

39) Tower Theater, 1926, S. Charles Lee, 800 SOUTH BROADWAY

39) On the left corner, the Tower Theater was L.A.'s first theater built for sound. The style combines Spanish, Romanesque, Moorish, and French elements. Clad in terra cotta with a corner clock tower, the structure was designed to create a theatrical experience on the exterior as well as inside. Notice the windows without glass and framed with Classical pediments. Scallop shell lighting provides the drama that lights up the movie theme images of actors and directors above the windows. Above, on the side of the building are recessed panels used for advertising, which would, no doubt, have been elaborately painted. S. Charles Lee became a well-known theater designer, who also designed the Max Factor Building in Hollywood. The building has been declared a Historic Cultural Monument by the City of Los Angeles.

40) The Rialto Theater has been re-mod-eled several times, but is still significant. In the 1980s it became a store. The marquee was one of the longest on Broadway, and has been de-clared a Historic Cultural Monument by the City of Los Angeles.

40) Rialto Theater, 1923, William Lee Woolett, 812 SOUTH BROADWAY

41) The Wurlitzer Building was the show-room for the famous organs, which provided the accompaniment for the silent films of the era. Designed in the Romanesque Revival style, the building features repeated arches and engaged col-umns decorated with diamond forms. It stands out with its white and green façade decorated with musical images of harps, horns, guitars and drums. Look above the first floor, which has been ob-scured and is not intact.

41) The Wurlitzer Building, c. 1918, A. Stanford, 818 SOUTH BROADWAY

42) Orpheum Theater, 1926, G. Albert Landsburg, 842 SOUTH BROADWAY

42) The Orpheum Theater was designed in the Beaux-Arts style, with a French themed in-terior. Lavish materials such as silk and marble are used on the main floor. The grand Wurlitzer or-gan in this theater is one of the last remaining on Broadway. The theater was completely restored in 2001 and is one of the few original theaters that is still used as it was originally intended. Fa-mous entertainers who have performed here in-clude the Marx Brothers, Lena Horne, Duke Ellington, and Count Basie. Judy Garland and Anne Miller were discovered here. The upper floors have been converted to apartments.

43) On the left is the Ninth & Broadway Building, in the Art Deco style, which was designed the same year and by the same architect as the Eastern Columbia Building directly across the street. Seen here are stylized floral forms, decorated spandrels and narrow piers that emphasize the vertical form of the building.

43) Ninth & Broadway Building, 1929, Claude Beelman, 830 South Broadway

44) Eastern Columbia Building (now 849 Building), 1929, Claude Beelman, 849 South Broadway

44) On your right, the turquoise and green glazed terra cotta Eastern Columbia Building is an excellent example of Art Deco Moderne. Eastern Outfitting and Columbia department stores were originally housed here. Notice the sunburst pattern in gold, and how the design spills out to the terrazzo sidewalk. The building stands out in the skyline because of its rich coloration. This building has been declared a Historic Cultural Monument by the City of Los Angeles.

45) On your right, the United Artists Theater was designed in the Spanish Gothic style, mostly characterized here by the pointed arches and tracery decoration. It was designed by the same architects who designed the Fine Arts Building and the Oviatt Building seen earlier. It was the first theater constructed by the United Artists Corporation as the only major preview house located in L.A. rather than in NYC. UA was formed by actors Charlie Chaplin, Mary Pickford, and Douglas Fairbanks, with director D.W. Griffith. The building has been declared a Historic Cultural Monument by the City of Los Angeles.

45) United Artists Theater, 1927, Walker & Eisen, 929 South Broadway

46) Further on your right is the magnificent Herald Examiner Building, designed by female architect Julia Morgan. She also designed Hearst Castle in San Simeon on the Central Coast of California for William Randolph Hearst, owner of the *Herald Examiner*. Architects J. Martyn Haenke and Dodd are credited with participation in this project as well. They may have prepared the working drawings and supervised construction. It was designed in the Spanish Colonial Revival style with Moorish details seen in the mosaic domes, combined with the Mission Revival style characterized by the flat central arched façade of the entrance. The building has been declared a Historic Cultural Monument by the City of Los Angeles.

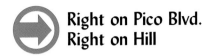

Right on Pico Blvd. Right on Hill

47) Here on your right are two theaters both designed by the same architects. The first is the Belasco Theater (now the Metropolitan Church), with some characteristics of the elaborate Spanish Churriguerresque style popular in the 1920s still visible. The building has been abandoned and declared a Historic Cultural Monument by the City of Los Angeles.

48) Next door is the Mayan Theater. Ancient Mayan architecture was the inspiration for this theater still in operation. Francisco Cornejo designed the elaborate decoration. When the theater opened in 1927 it was painted gray in an attempt to make it look like an ancient Mayan building. Images of Mayan warriors are depicted above the marquee. The design is also carried out on the interior. In 1989 it was restored and is currently a thriving performance space and nightclub. The building has been declared a Historic Cultural Monument by the City of Los Angeles.

46) Herald Examiner Building, 1912, Julia Morgan, 1111 SOUTH BROADWAY

47) Belasco Theater (now Metropolitan Church), 1926, Morgan, Walls & Clements, 1060 SOUTH HILL STREET

48) Mayan Theatre, 1927, Morgan, Walls & Clements, 1040 SOUTH HILL STREET

48) Mayan Theatre, 1927, Morgan, Walls & Clements, 1040 SOUTH HILL STREET

49) Skyline

Right on Olympic

50) Now you are going through the Fashion District, California Mart, and the Produce Mart – a very active area concerned with every-day commerce in Los Angeles.

50) Fashion District, California Mart, and Produce Mart.

Right on San Julian
Left on Pico
Right on San Pedro
Left on 14th Place
Left on Central Avenue

51) The Coca-Cola Bottling Company Plant building is a veritable replica of an ocean liner, complete with a bridge, portholes, riveted construction, and a water line painted on the exterior. The building was designed by the same architect who designed the "Crossroads of the World" office complex on Sunset Blvd. in Hollywood. In the 1930s, Art Deco architecture morphed into the Streamline Moderne style expressed here as a result of the Great Depression, and was much more pared-down with much less surface decoration. This is an excellent example of the Late Art Deco style. The growing interest in the automobile, air travel, and ocean liner cruises by the wealthy was also influential in the evolution of this style. There were smaller buildings on the site originally, and this new one served to wrap them all together. The building has been declared a Historic Cultural Monument by the City of Los Angeles.

51) Coca-Cola Bottling Company Plant, 1937, Robert Derrah, 1334 SOUTH CENTRAL AVENUE

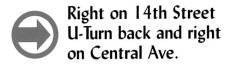

Right on 14th Street U-Turn back and right on Central Ave.

52) Across the street is the Engine Company No. 30. Designed for the City of Los Angeles just after the turn of the century for $500, it was the first African American fire department. Some elements of the Beaux-Arts style can be seen here in the scrolled brackets and acanthus foliage. Now a museum, the building has been declared a Historic Cultural Monument by the City of Los Angeles.

52) Engine Company No. 30 LAFD Truck No. 11, c.1913, J.J. Backus, Restored 1997, Edward H. Fickett, 1401 SOUTH CENTRAL AVENUE

53) On your right is the Seventh Street Market (produce) at 784 South Central Avenue. It is the wholesale produce market where most of the activity takes place in the early morning.

53) Seventh Street Market (produce), 784 SOUTH CENTRAL AVENUE

Continue on Central Avenue

54) Higashi Honganji Buddhist Temple, 1976, Kajima Associates, 505 EAST 3RD STREET

You are now entering Little Tokyo with its beginnings in the early 1900s. Many Japanese came to Los Angeles from San Francisco after the 1906 earthquake. They came here as business people and opened their own shops, drugstores, restaurants, and other establishments.

54) On the left corner is the Higashi Honganji Buddhist Temple, inspired by the Todaiji in Nara, Japan. The massive, steeply sloped roof is covered with more than 3,000 tiles from Japan. The roofline flares at the end in the traditional style. The two fish at the top of the roof are water symbols set there to protect against fires. Inside, the traditional style continues.

Map Five

PERSHING SQUARE

LITTLE TOKYO

Grand Av

6th St

Olive St

Hill St

Broadway

Spring St

Main St

Los Angeles St

4th St

3rd St

2nd St

1st St

59

58

57

55

56

3rd St

Traction Ave

Alameda St

Santa e

Center St

1st St

Central Av

4th St

4th St

Mateo St

9th St

Flower St

Hope St

Olympic Bl

11th St

Wall St

Maple St

6th St

7th St

San Pedro St

5th St

Crocker St

8th St

San Julian St

Stanford Av

Ceres Av

9th St

Wall St

Olympic Bl

10

11th St

San Julian St

Olympic Bl

12th St

Pico Bl

Crocker St

Stanford Av

Olive St

Hill St

Broadway

Main St

Los Angeles St

Venice Bl

Santa Monica

6th St

7th St

10

56) Freight Depot, 1907, Harrison Albright, (now Southern California Institute of Architecture, SCI-ARC), Remodeled 2001 Gary Paige Studio & Sci-Arc Alumni, 960 East 3rd Street

 Right on 2nd Street
Right on Hewitt

55) On your left, The Maryknoll Japanese Catholic Center was designed in the Spanish Romanesque style with terra cotta pipe roofing. Notice how the shape of the roof flares slightly at the ends, a feature which alludes to Japanese architecture. The church was established in Los Angeles in 1912 by a Japanese-speaking French missionary named Father Alfred Breton. The Maryknoll Fathers came in 1921 after two Victorian mansions were moved from the site to make room for the establishment of the church. There is also a school in back that was built in 1964 and was staffed by the Maryknoll sisters. The Franciscan Friars of Atonement have been administering the church since 1997 and continue to do so with a congregation of approximately 3,000 congregants.

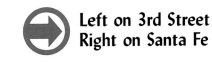 **Left on 3rd Street**
Right on Santa Fe

56) On your right is the Freight Depot (now SCI-ARC), which was originally a train depot for the Atchison, Topeka, and Santa Fe Railways. Notice the train station across the street on the left. This is an excellent example of an adaptive re-use of a structure where the building remains virtually intact, yet is used for something other than for what it was originally intended. SCI-ARC, formed in 1972 and originally located in Santa Monica, is Los Angeles' progressive architecture school. Its opening in 2001 has helped to revitalize this area.

55) Maryknoll Japanese Catholic Center, St. Francis Xavier Chapel, c. 1938, (architect unknown), 222 South Hewitt Street

You are now going through part of the Artist's District and part of the Toy District.

➡️ **Go under the bridge
Turn right onto Molino
Keep turning right
onto Molino then
Straight across at 4th
Left on Traction
Right on Alameda
Left on 1st Street**

**Look down between the two
buildings to your right and you
will see amidst all of this:**

57) On your right is the Japanese American National Museum. This is the heart of Little Tokyo, and this very recent museum creates a reflection of the older structure across the street, which was a Buddhist temple and the former home of the museum.

58) The Geffen Contemporary at MOCA, another branch of the museum seen earlier. Frank Gehry remodeled an existing warehouse by incorporating ramps and steps leading to a second level with large doors in order to make the moving of large sculpture easy. It is an enormous box that can be transformed to suit various exhibitions.

57) Japanese American National Museum, 1925, Edgar Cline, Remodeled 1992 KNSU Joint Venture Architects, 119 NORTH CENTRAL AVENUE

58) The Geffen Contemporary at MOCA, 1983, Frank O. Gehry and Associates, 152 NORTH CENTRAL AVENUE

Left on Los Angeles Street

59) On your right, St. Vibiana's Cathedral was modeled after the Church of San Miguel in Barcelona. It is Victorian-era Italianate in style. Badly aged and damaged by the 6.8, 1994 Northridge earthquake, it has recently been the subject of controversy, but was saved from demolition by the Los Angeles Conservancy. Developer Tom Gilmore has come to the rescue and purchased it, and it will be become another example of adaptive re-use as it becomes a performance space for California State University, Los Angeles. Directly in front of the church is the Little Tokyo branch of the Los Angeles library. Designed by architect Anthony J. Lumsden, completed in 2004, it houses the library's largest collection of Japanese language materials. Of low, horizontal form, it's design is inspired by Japanese architecture, yet reflective of the early work of Frank Lloyd Wright and R.M. Schindler. St. Vibiana's Cathedral has been declared a Historic Cultural Monument by the City of Los Angeles.

59) St. Vibiana's Cathedral, 1876, Ezra Kysor & W. J. Matthews, Renovated 1922, John C. Austin, 114 EAST 2ND STREET

Right on 5th Street
Right on Hill Street

61) Here at the far right corner is the Title Guarantee & Trust Company Building, designed by the same architects who created Union Station and many other buildings Downtown, as well as Bullock's Wilshire in the Miracle Mile. It is in the late Art Deco ZigZag Moderne style. There are, however, flying buttresses at the top, reminiscent of the Gothic style. The building has been declared a Historic Cultural Monument by the City of Los Angeles. It is also listed on the National Register of Historic Places.

62) Subway Terminal Building, 1926, Schultze & Weaver, Restored 1986, Brenda Levin & Associates, 417 SOUTH HILL STREET

60) Another view of Pershing Square. Notice the pink truncated columns.

61) Title Guarantee & Trust Company Building, 1931, John & Donald Parkinson, 401-411 WEST 5TH STREET

62) On the left again is the Subway Terminal Building, now seen from the front. The structure was designed by Schultze & Weaver, the same architects who designed the Biltmore Hotel. It was later restored in 1986 by Levin & Associates. It uses the same separation of the four bay sections, based upon a 16th century Italian structure. There were five subway tracks underneath and the tunnel was a mile in length. At its peak use in 1944, 844 trains of the Pacific Electric Railway carried some 65,000 passengers daily. Notice the tromp l'oeuil windows above. This building has been declared a Historic Cultural Monument by the City of Los Angeles.

The slender glass tower to the left of the building is part of the original telephone company building, Pacific Bell, now AT & T and SBC.

63) Up the hill on the left is Angel's Flight, a funicular train designed to bring passengers up and down Bunker Hill. It was often called "the world's shortest railway." Two cars named Olivet and Sinai ran on a counterweight system and took fifty seconds to complete a one-way trip. The train was originally located further down the street next to the tunnel until it was moved to this location when it was restored. It was dismantled in 1969 and put in storage until its restoration. In 2001 there was a terrible accident and someone was killed, and it has not yet reopened. This structure has been declared a Historic Cultural Monument by the City of Los Angeles. It is also listed on the National Register of Historic Places.

63) Angel's Flight, 1901, Restored 1996, Tetra Design, 351 South Hill Street

64) California Plaza, 1980, Arthur Erickson Architects, Kamnitzer & Cotton, Gruen Associates, 300 and 350 South Grand Avenue

64) At the top of the hill beyond Angel's Flight is the tall, glass-clad California Plaza, a typical high-rise office building. There are some interesting fountains in the plaza. Bunker Hill was once a very desirable neighborhood to live in, with elaborate Victorian mansions owned by the wealthiest people in the city, including the Bradbury family. These homes have all been demolished or moved elsewhere.

65) On your right is the Grand Central Public Market, the oldest market in the city. It offers a wide variety of ethnic foods with fifty-eight separate market stalls. In the exterior corner is an inverted clock created by artist Tim Hawkinson.

65) Grand Central Public Market, 1898, (architect unknown), Restored 1987-1995 Levin & Associates, South Hill Street

66) View of tunnel under Bunker Hill and Disney Hall above.

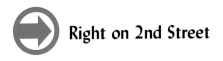 **Right on 2nd Street**

67) The third location for the newspaper, The Los Angeles Times Building was designed in the Late Art Deco style. It is serious, with graceful, strong lines and no elaborate surface decoration, as was popular in the 1930s Late Art Deco style. There are some very interesting spaces inside, including the Globe Lobby, where an enormous marble globe rotates with a backdrop mu-

ral by Hugo Ballin titled, "Newspaper." The newer building constructed in 1970 by William Pereira and Associates is more like a Mies Van der Rohe-inspired Modernist box, with multi-level parking on the side. No attempt was made for the new building to blend in with the older building.

67) Los Angeles Times Building, 1931-35, Gordon Kaufmann, Expansion 1970, William Pereira & Associates, 202 WEST 1ST STREET

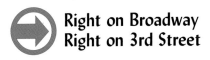 **Right on Broadway Right on 3rd Street**

68) On the left corner is the Bradbury Building. Bradbury made his fortune in gold mining and wanted to leave a legacy as he approached the end of his life. He decided to build a great monumental building and approached the well-known architect Sumner Hunt, but did not like his design. He ended up hiring a draftsman in Hunt's office, and the result was a truly magnificent building. Unfortunately, he died before the building was completed. The exterior is very different from the interior and gives no indication of what is inside. A warm and graceful interior, there are skylights, balconies, and a hand-operated elevator in a cage. The building features cast-iron railings and yellow glazed tiled walls with offices oriented around an interior wrap-around balcony. Used in numerous movies including "Blade Runner" and "Wolf," the building has been declared a Historic Cultural Monument by the City of Los Angeles. It is also listed on the National Register of Historic Places.

68) Bradbury Building, 1893, George Wyman, Restored 1991,
Levin & Associates. 304 SOUTH BROADWAY

69) Directly across from the Bradbury Building is the elaborate Million Dollar Theatre opened by Hollywood-famous Sid Grauman. The building was said to have cost a million dollars to build. Decorated with bison heads and eagles as symbols of the West, and images of the theatrical arts. It was converted to residential lofts in 1988.

69) Million Dollar Theatre, 1918, A.C. Martin, William L. Woolett,
307 SOUTH BROADWAY

Map Seven

Right on Hill Street

70) Again, on your left is the Los Angeles County Courthouse. Visible from this angle is the relief sculpture above the entry depicting "Justice."

70)Los Angeles County Courthouse, 1958, J.E. Stanton, Paul Williams, Adrian Wilson, Austin, Field and Fry, CORNER HILL & 1ST

71) On your right, the Hall of Records Building is a unique example of a high-rise office building by Modernist architect Richard Neutra and others. The vertical louvers shielding the glass window wall emphasize the height of the building and are an element that Neutra used on his own home.

71) Hall of Records Building, 1962, Richard Neutra, Robert Alexander, Honnold & Rex, Herman Charles Light, and James Friend, 320 WEST TEMPLE STREET

72) On the left is the Hahn Hall of Administration housing civic offices and part of the county courts complex. The three columns of squared window openings mark the side entrance.

72) Hahn Hall of Administration, 1961, J.E. Stanton, Paul Williams, Adrian Wilson, Austin, Field, and Fry, 225 NORTH HILL STREET

73) On the left at the corner is one of L.A.'s most recently-completed buildings, the Cathedral of Our Lady of the Angels. The Los Angeles archdiocese is the largest in the United States. The design for the cathedral was chosen from a design competition of 55 submissions. From this vantage point you can see the administrative offices and clergy residences. (Later you will drive on the other side of the building and see the front entrance.) The exterior material is concrete, resembling large-scale clapboard siding, the color of which is reminiscent of the adobe of the missions. This cathedral was intended to reflect the Spanish heritage of southern California. Large windows throughout faced on the interior with alabaster stone allow indirect light to enter the building. The design concept for the building was "Light and Journey," and on the approach to the main sanctuary is a long hallway with chapels on the right side. Some are empty and will be filled over time. The bells at the front entrance are from St. Monica's church, while some of the chandeliers and stained glass are from St. Vibiana's. In the basement level is a large crypt, where Gregory Peck and others are buried, and where space can be purchased. Artwork was created by local artists, such as the outdoor fountain by Lita Albuquerque, a tapestry by John Nava, and the enormous bronze doors by noted-sculptor Robert Graham. On the back side is the Shrine of Guadalupe, which overlooks the freeway, and a glass wall etched with images of angels. Docent-lead tours are available and recommended.

73) Cathedral of Our Lady of the Angels, 2002, Jose Rafael Moneo (design architect) with Leo A. Daly (executive architect and engineer), 555 WEST TEMPLE STREET

Continue on Hill Street

74) On your left, on the overpass of the freeway is the Fort Moore Pioneer Memorial. The Fort, which was once at this site, was the city's first U.S. Military fort. It was named for Captain Benjamin Moore, who in 1846 took a lance through the heart in one of the few battles of the Mexican-American war. This memorial celebrates the importation of water to L.A. and the completion of the California Aqueduct. It reads, "May those who live in our naturally arid land be thankful for the vision and good works of the pioneer leaders of Los Angeles, and may all in their time ever provide for its citizens water and power for life and energy." This was also a memorial for the Mormon soldiers who fought in the war. It originally had a 50-foot high and 70-foot long waterfall.

74) Fort Moore, 1957, Fountain Relief, Henry Kreis, Albert Stewart, Pioneer Memorial, 1957, HILL STREET OVERPASS

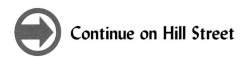 **Continue on Hill Street**

You will be entering Chinatown soon. Chinatown had its beginnings in the 1850s where Union Station now stands. The Chinese made up the largest labor force in California in the mid-19th century, and many of them came here to partake in the riches of the California Gold Rush. Chinese workers also came to southern California to build the railroads. In 1869 the Transcontinental Railroad was completed. In 1870 there were about 200 Chinese here and the area became known as Chinatown. In 1900 thousands of Chinese lived here in ghetto conditions. This was all demolished to make way for Union Station in 1933. The "New Chinatown", which is what now exists, was built here and opened in 1938.

According to census records, besides Chinese, immigrants from France, Germany, Italy, and even Syria all lived here in the early 1900s. Approximately 15,000 people now live in Chinatown, where Latinos represent twenty percent of the population, which is dominated by 10,000 Chinese. The Chinese population has shifted to a new area in Monterey Park and San Gabriel further east.

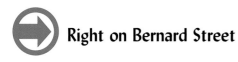 **Right on Bernard Street**

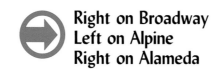 **Right on Broadway**
Left on Alpine
Right on Alameda

77) On the left, the Terminal Annex Post Office was designed in the Spanish Colonial Revival style with Moorish details, characterized by the colorful mosaic domes on either side.

75) The Chinese Historical Society moved here in 1995 into two very modest Victorian houses, which were originally owned by French immigrant Philip Fritz. Housed here are historical records and photos, and contemporary art exhibitions. In the late 1990s they received a gift of 200,000 artifacts dating back to the earlier settlers. They were collected at 50 digs in the area during the construction of the Metro Red Line, completed in 1999. The Society offers walking tours of Chinatown.

76) On your right is Philippe's The Original Restaurant. Here since 1908, it is famous for its meat sandwiches dipped in juice, which were created by accident. The legend says that on a particular day, one of the sandwiches was dipped in the meat juices because the bread was slightly stale. It was served to a hungry gentleman who liked it so much that he returned the next day and asked that the sandwich be dipped in the juice again. The French dip sandwich has become an L.A. institution.

77) Terminal Annex Post Office, 1938, (architect unknown), 900 NORTH ALAMEDA AVENUE

 Left on Cesar Chavez
Right on Vignes Street

75) Chinese Historical Society, 1886, 415 BERNARD STREET

76) Philippe's The Original Restaurant, 1908, 1001 NORTH ALAMEDA STREET

78) The Towers Correctional Facility (a.k.a. Jail) situated on the outskirts of Downtown, yet close enough to the courthouses for processing. The geometric block forms create an imposing presence, and the severely narrow, slit windows indicate the building's purpose. Light can get in, but no one can get out.

79) The Patsaouras Transit Plaza is the new terminal for the Metro Rail Line, L.A.'s new (c. 1999) underground rail system. Inside there is an array of art by local artists with the theme of the history of Los Angeles or transportation. This building connects to Union Station in back of it. The Transit Plaza was named for Greek immigrant Nick Patsouras, who was instrumental in developing L.A's transit system.

79) Patsaouras Transit Plaza, (Metro Center), 2000, Ehrenkrantz, Ekstut Architects, MVP Architects, 1 GATEWAY PLAZA

78) The Towers Correctional Facility, c.1990s, (architect unknown), 450 BAUCHET STREET

Right onto the freeway ramp
Right onto the freeway

Take first exit for Alameda St./Union Station Turn right on Alameda

80) On your left, the grayish building across the freeway is the Los Angeles Metropolitan Detention Center. Quite a contemporary-looking jail, again with narrow, slit windows. The horizontal bridges visually connect the massing of the vertical forms, and the metal superstructure above provides security.

81) On your right is Union Station, the major train station for Los Angeles, designed in a combination of the Spanish Mission and the Streamline Moderne styles popular in the 1930s, by the same architects who designed other Downtown buildings, as well as the Bullock's Wilshire department store on Wilshire Blvd.. The huge arched windows in front, white surface, clock tower, and terra cotta pipe roof give it a Mediterranean feeling. Inside its massive spaces, the oversized leather chairs and dark decorative tiling create an impressive setting. The building conveys both a sense of tradition and modernity, and has been used in numerous films, including "The Way We Were," "True Confessions," and "To Live and Die in L.A." The building has been declared a Historic Cultural Monument by the City of Los Angeles. It is also listed on the National Register of Historic Places.

81) Union Station, 1939, John & Donald Parkinson, 800 NORTH ALAMEDA STREET

80) Los Angeles Metropolitan Detention Center, 1988, Ellerbe Becket/Louis Naidorf, 635 NORTH ALAMEDA STREET

Map Eight

Drive through the station and straight out to Los Angeles St. Find a parking spot

82) On your right are Olvera Street and El Pueblo De Los Angeles, which are really best seen on foot as some of the sites are hidden from the car's view on pedestrian streets. It is recommended that you walk this area.

Olvera Street and El Pueblo De Los Angeles make up the true historic core of the city. This is where the Spanish sent eleven families from Sonora, Mexico to found the city in 1781. The area consists of a number of significant buildings; including the oldest building in Los Angeles. This was the center of the city for many years. Many of the buildings have been restored and are now open to the public. The area is listed as a Historic Cultural Monument by the City of Los Angeles. It is also listed on the National Register of Historic Places.

83) La Iglesia de Nuestra Senora la Reina de Los Angeles, one of the oldest churches in the city, was built by New England native Joseph Chapman. He was recruited by the Franciscan fathers to build ships and buildings. It has been re-modeled many times, but the style most closely resembles the Spanish Mission style. The church is still an important gathering place for the Catholic population in this area. The building has been declared a Historic Cultural Monument by the City of Los Angeles.

83) La Iglesia de Nuestra Señora la Reina de Los Angeles, 1822, Joseph Chapman, 535 NORTH MAIN STREET

82) Olvera Street and El Pueblo De Los Angeles.

 Walk down the pedestrian-only street on the east (right) side of the Plaza, next to the Mexican Cultural Institute

The Avila Adobe is the city's oldest dwelling, c. 1818, at 10 Olvera Street. (It is only visible from the pedestrian street and is now a public museum.) The house was in disrepair in the 1920s and was going to be demolished, however, it was saved from the wrecking ball and restored only to suffer more damaged in the 1971 earthquake, after which it was rebuilt in concrete. It is a good example of early California life.

84) The Pico House, originally a hotel, was built during the Victorian era in the Italiante style, with its arched façade. This style was more typical in the East and Midwest. The building was named after Pio Pico, who was the last Mexican governor of California. It is now houses offices. Kysor also designed St. Vibiana's cathedral seen earlier.

84) Pico House, 1870, Attributed to Ezra Kysor, OLVERA STREET

85) The Old Plaza Firehouse has been recently restored and is now a public museum. It was also built during the Victorian era.

85) Old Plaza Firehouse, 1884, (architect unknown), LOS ANGELES STREET

86) The Garnier Block, built by Philippe Garnier, is a two-story brick and stone structure with Romanesque styling. This is the only remaining edifice from the original Chinatown. The Garnier Block of offices was constructed specifically for Chinese businesses. This was once a residence and meeting place for Chinese immigrants, and has recently been restored and opened as the Chinese-American Museum.

86) Garnier Block, Chinese-American Museum, 1890, 415 NORTH LOS ANGELES STREET

 Cross the freeway and continue on Los Angeles Street

87) The Los Angeles Mall, completed in 1974 and consists of some underground shops and an underground parking lot. It once housed the Children's Museum and City Hall East, which are no longer here. This is also the site of the city's first newspaper, the *Los Angeles Star* and is very near the original Native American village that Spanish explorers came upon in 1769. Fletcher Bowron Square was named for a progressive 20th century mayor.

87) Los Angeles Mall, 1974, Fletcher Bowron Square, Stanton & Stockwell, 225 NORTH LOS ANGELES STREET

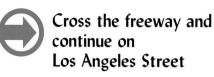 **Right on Temple Street**

88) On your left is the recently restored Los Angeles City Hall. Austin was responsible for the working drawings and the administration of the project, Parkinson developed the concept and design, and Martin created the structural design. Some of the best architects of the time collaborated on this important building, combining different forms of architecture with a step pyramid at the very top. The building is supported by a tall skyscraper shaft and a horizontal base. The exterior is comprised of terra cotta blocks manufactured by Gladding McBean. City Hall was the tallest building in Los Angeles at 452 feet until the 1960s. The Lindbergh Beacon, a 1,000-watt light at the top of the pyramid, was first lit in 1928. The city officials asked Charles Lindbergh, who had completed his Atlantic crossing one year before, for recommendations regarding the city's tallest building, and he suggested doing something that would help aviators find L.A. The light, however, was turned off during World War II, but was restored and will now be used for special occasions. The interior is Spanish Colonial Revival, Romanesque and Byzantine-inspired with an elaborate use of marble and a central rotunda. The dedication in 1928 was planned by Sid Grauman, known for his elaborate movie premiere promotions. Part of the restoration included lifting the building and placing it on base isolators to make it resistant to earthquakes. The building has been declared a Historic Cultural Monument by the City of Los Angeles.

88) Los Angeles City Hall, 1928, John C. Austin, John and Donald Parkinson, and Albert C. Martin, Restored 2001 A.C. Martin & Associates, Levin & Associates, 200 NORTH MAIN STREET (200 NORTH SPRING STREET)

89) On the right corner here is the Federal Building and Post Office (now the U.S. Federal Courthouse). A very sober, serious building, it is faced in granite and has a flat, box shape. Square windows frame the vertical bands of windows, creating a strong wall façade that's alludes to Classicism, but is really an abstraction. The Classical fluted columns on the ground floor mark the entrance. This building was very well-liked when it was first built.

89) Federal Building and Post Office (now U.S. Federal Courthouse), 1940, Louis A. Simon, Gilbert Stanley Underwood, 312 NORTH SPRING STREET

90) Hall of Justice, 1925, Allied Architects, CORNER OF SOUTH BROADWAY AND TEMPLE STREETS

90) On the right is the Hall of Justice. Sheathed in gray granite with Classical columns above, it is Italian Renaissance Revival in style. This location has been the site of conflict resolution since the 1870s, when there were shootouts, gang wars, and lynchings. Of course, many famous people have been through the Hall of Justice, including Errol Flynn, Charlie Chaplin, Bugsy Siegel, Charles Manson, and Robert Mitchum. Marilyn Monroe's autopsy took place here. Housed in the present Italian Renaissance structure were offices for the coroner, district attorney, and public defender, in addition to courtrooms, jail cells, and a morgue. As newer buildings in the area of the Civic Center were being built in the 1960s and 1970s, the offices here moved out. The Northridge earthquake in 1994 was the last nail in the coffin of the building, when it was declared unsafe. It is currently abandoned, although there are plans for a restoration that should be completed in 2005 and will house the sheriff's office.

90a) You will see the Cathedral, Music Center, Department of Water and Power, Criminal Courts Building, Board of Supervisors of Los Angeles County, and County of Los Angeles Health Services Administration on Temple Street.

Now you will go to the outskirts of downtown and into the first suburb of Los Angeles, Angelino Heights.

90a)Cathedral of Our Lady of the Angels, 2002, Jose Rafael Moneo (design architect) with Leo A. Daly (executive architect and engineer), 555 WEST TEMPLE STREET

Map Nine

101
2

2

Temple St

ECHO
PARK

ECHO PARK
LAKE/REC.
CENTER

Park Av

Park Av

Kellam Ave 91

Caroll Ave 92

96 93

95 94

Douglas St

Edgeware Rd

Elysian Park Av

DODGER
STADIUM

Lilac Ter

Stadium Wy

LAKE

Lake St

Alvarado St

Court St

Beverly Bl

Glendale Bl

Edgeware Rd 97

101

Hollywood Fwy

Sunset Bl

Pasadena Fwy

110

College St

Alpine St

ARTHUR

Bonnie Brae St

3rd St

Union Av

Douglas St

Court St

Temple St

Figueroa Bl

Cesar Chavez Av

Grand Av

EL PUEBLO
DE LOS ANGELES
HISTORIC
MONUMENT

BI

Lucas Av

Beaudry Av

1st St

Hope St

CIVIC
CENTER

Grand Ave

N. Hill St

N. Broadway

➡ **Continue on Temple Street**
Right on Edgeware Road
Left on Bellevue Avenue
Right on Douglas Street
Right on Kellam Avenue

On this street are a number of Victorian-era houses, some of which have been moved to this area for reasons of preservation. Kellam Avenue and Carroll Avenue have a large concentration of homes built during the late Victorian Period from the 1870s to the 1900s. (The Victorian period started approximately during the late 1830s.) Typical of the time were designs with varied surface textures, clapboard siding, gingerbread wood decoration, Classical details, columns, pilasters, pediments, decorated friezes, towers, turrets, and porches. The term "Victorian" is from England and was well-suited to the economic boom of the time as a symbol of wealth and success, as it alluded to neo-Classical elements associated with the upper classes of Europe. From 1833 the Industrial Age was raging, and the work of craftsmen was disappearing, replaced by what the machine could manufacture. Many of the elements of Victorian architecture are a reflection of this phenomenon. Pattern books outlining the style could be purchased. These were used to build the houses, so often there was no architect associated with the design of the house. This area was declared a Historic Preservation Overlay Zone (HPOZ) in 1981 by the City of Los Angeles. It was the first such zone to be created here. There are now fifteen HPOZs throughout the city. The 1300 block of Carroll Avenue is also listed on the National Register of Historic Places.

91) The three-story Queen Anne style house on the corner sits high on its site. On the third story you'll see rounded fish scale shingles, and pointed fish scale shingles on the second story. The sunburst design in the triangular pediment above the entry is a typical Victorian decorative element, as are the turned wood columns that flank the entry. On both the first and second floors are protruding bay windows. All of these elements are characteristic of the Queen Anne style.

92) Further down the street on the right is a modest one-and-a-half story house with three dormers, one with a porthole window. Supporting the porch are single, double, and triple columns on bases. The frieze above is decorated with swags of garlands, and horizontal clapboard siding was used. This is also of the Queen Anne style, however, the heavy columns in front are Colonial Revival style.

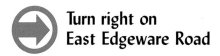

Turn right on East Edgeware Road

93) On your left, the two-and-a-half story polychrome pastel painted house is very different from the rest. The shape is not as rectilinear as the others. Rather, it is more geometric with its faceted tower and dormers on the left crowned by a decorative iron crest that meets the sky. The wrap-around porch with turned wood spindle railing and the clapboard siding is, however, more typical.

91) House, c.1887, (architect unknown), 1347 AND 1349 KELLAM AVENUE

92) House, 1890, (architect unknown), 1334 KELLAM AVENUE

93) House, 1887, (architect unknown), 724 NORTH EAST EDGEWARE ROAD

Right on Carroll Avenue

94) On your left, the three-story house is full of Queen Anne details. The corner tower on the left of the house, rounded turret on the right with conical roof, wrap-around porch with turned spindles for the railing, and fan decoration on the front door and under the windows are all characteristic of the Queen Anne style. The physical shape of the house, with its protrusions and bays, is tied together by the exterior decoration.

94) Heim House, 1888, (architect unknown), 1320 CARROLL AVENUE

95) Two doors down on your left is the Sessions House, the most elaborate house in the neighborhood. This home is another example of Queen Anne Victorian architecture, with some Chinese detailing seen in the circular "moongate." Wood latticework, fish scale shingles, a wrap-around porch and the sunburst pattern in the triangular pediment are all characteristics of this high style. This was the home of the dairy owner Charles W. Sessions.

95) Sessions House, 1880, Joseph Cather Newsom, 1330 CARROLL AVENUE

96) Across the street on the right is the Innes House, in the Eastlake style (also known as Stick style). Charles Eastlake was a British interior designer and author who wrote on style and good taste. This style proliferated from 1880-1890 and had a very different feeling than the others. It was more "squared-off" in appearance with rectilinear forms and horizontal plain clapboard siding. The applied trim was incised with decoration on the windows and doors. The rectangular windows were framed by stained glass squares, creating a more serious and straightforward feeling.

96) Innes House, 1888, (architect unknown), 1329 CARROLL AVENUE

Left on Douglas Street
Left on Bellevue
Right on Edgeware Road

97) On the left is the Vista Angelina Housing, built more than one hundred years after its neighbors across the street. This apartment complex was designed to resemble and honor the original Victorian buildings in the neighborhood. The siding, colors, and iron cresting at the top are similar to the houses of the neighborhood, creating a visual connection between the present and the past.

97) Vista Angelina Housing, 1994, Birba Group, 418 NORTH EAST EDGEWARE ROAD

Left on Temple towards Downtown
right on Grand Avenue and back to MOCA

SELECTED BIBLIOGRAPHY

Gebhard, David, and Robert Winter. *Los Angeles: An Architectural Guide*. Layton, Utah: Gibbs Smith Publisher, 1994.

Gleye, Paul. *The Architecture of Los Angeles*. Los Angeles: Rosebud Books-The Knapp Press, 1981.

Herr, Jeffrey, ed.. *Landmark L.A.: Historic-Cultural Monuments of Los Angeles*. City of Los Angeles Cultural Affairs Department, Santa Monica, California: Angel City Press, 2002.

Kaplan, Sam Hall. *L.A. Lost and Found: An Architectural History of Los Angeles*. New York: Crown Publishers, 1987.

McGrew, Patrick and Julian, Robert. *Landmarks of Los Angeles*. New York: Harry N. Abrams Publishers, 1994.

Steele, James. *Los Angeles Architecture. The Contemporary Condition*. London, England: Phaidon Press, Ltd., 1993.

Index of Architects